PRIVATE EYE

OXFORD BOOK OF PSEUDS

Illustrated by Kathryn Lamb

PRIVATE EYE

First published in 1983 by
Private Eye Productions Limited
34 Greek Street, London W1.

© Pressdram Limited

ISBN 233 97586 1

Also available:
Book of Pseuds
Second Book of Pseuds

Filmset by
Metro Reprographics Ltd. London

Printed in Great Britain by
Butler & Tanner Ltd., Frome and London

CONTENTS

OVERTURE

It was in October 1982 over lunch at Victor Sassie's famous Hungarian restaurant *The Gay Hussar* that I first asked Christopher Logue if he would like to compile a new collection of Pseuds; to complete, in other words, the unfinished triptych already comprising *The Book of Pseuds* (1973) and *The Psecond Book of Pseuds* (1977). Gazing thoughtfully across the restaurant to where an Italian countess was at that moment raising a morsel of braised partridge to her exquisite lips, Logue replied, in that light, rasping voice of his, so redolent of the satirical cabaret of the early Sixties: "How much do I get?"

One sensed immediately in that, at first sight, down to earth query the philosophic astringency which so much appealed to T.S. Elliot when he first met the young Logue in 1958. Elliot later referred in his diary to "a poet who has pared life and language to its symbolic essence – who is not afraid to pose the salient question". Thus, to borrow Elliot's critique, we can see that the apparently mundane query "How much do I get?" applies not so much to matters of monetary reward as to the predicament of mankind in the universe.

How much do we get? No-one can be sure of the answer.

I would like therefore to thank Christopher Logue for agreeing to assemble this pungent pot-pourri.

R.I
Malmö,
Sweden

HORS D'OEUVRES

The Sixties were an oyster decade: slippery, luxurious and reportedly aphrodisiac they slipped down the historical throat without touching the sides.

Julian Barnes, The Observer

In the 1960s, the apologetics of leisure arose. The polymorphous perverse was enthroned, the puritan ethic discounted.

Malcolm Bradbury, The Observer

ART

... this book is as full of easily assimilable gossip as it is of absurd mistakes. Of the latter I shall bother only to correct the glaring mis-statement that the work of the remarkable French painter Francis Gruber is unknown outside France, for I well recall attending the Tate Gallery's retrospective exhibition of his work in the company of his widow, the daughter of the famous playwright Henri Bernstein.

Alistair Forbes, Spectator

Edward Weston rejected exotic subject matter in favour of the mundane – in Mexico for instance he photographed his lavatory bowl which, he said, 'reminded me in the glory of its swelling, sweeping, forward movement of finely progressing contours, of the Winged Victory of Samothrace'.

Sarah Kent, Time Out

When asked to say what I do, which is always a difficult question, I say that I make artefacts and usually talk about ritual, I think ritual has a lot to do with the way I work. I'm involved in an elongated ritual. It's a banal process but even the most banal activity takes on a new meaning when approached with the right attitude.

Alistair Wilson

A naked woman is being paid with rate-payers' money . . . to writhe in a pile of clay at an art show.

Mona Hatoum, a Lebanese artist, will perform for three hours at the exhibition in Portsmouth, Hants.

Art gallery spokesman Steve Chettle said: "The symbolism involved is important. "Being naked is evidence of isolation and the clay deepens the sense of oppression she feels as a woman and possibly as a Lebanese."

The Sun

Then there was Phillip Guston who was once a much-respected Abstract Impressionist but who spent the last few years of his life painting scratch and sniff pictures which smelled of stale vodka and cigarettes, old spunk and dirty sheets. Guston gave the impression of someone who lost his shame at around the same time as he lost his razor. I found his art gloriously liberating.

Waldemar Januszcek, Guardian

His best paintings have the same relaxed but taut economy of behaviour as a sailor on shore leave.

Bryan Robertson, Spectator

BIRTHS & DEATHS

BOHANNON – On August 12th at Queen Charlotte's Hospital Kathryn (neè Macpherson) Bohannon and Benton Porterfield Bohannon Jnr joyfully announce the birth of their son Benton Porterfield Bohannon III.

The Times (births column)

OBITUARY
Lady Anne Fleming
I remember her best, away from her gilded world, either hunting for plovers' eggs in an Orkney bog, or for maidenhead fern on the cliffs of Moher, or stalking wild goats above Mycenae . . .

Patrick Trevor-Roper, Tatler

BOOKS

THE SACRED AND THE FEMININE
Towards a Theology of Housework
by Kathryn Allen Rabuzzi

New York Review

Migrations is set (perhaps?) in South London. A man walks down a deserted street. It is night. He falters, then falls. A man looks down into the sunlit street. Is it the same man? Who is he? Why is he there? The novel explores these questions in a book about consciousness, identity, refuge, and pain. This is undoubtedly Gabriel Josipovici's most important and striking book.

Advertisement – Bookseller

The influence of the parents' power relationships on the gender of the sauna stove in a child's imagination

by Olli Ihalainen, and Eeva-Liisa Helkala, Psychiatria Fennica

THE TAO OF POOH Benjamin Hoff Illustrated by Ernest Shepard.

The bear of little brain has a certain 'way' about him. Benjamin Hoff examines this 'way' and proves that Pooh's way of life is amazingly consistent with the principles of Taoism. A must for all Pooh fans.

*Books for Christmas
IBS Information Service*

BOOTLICKERS

Aspinall's sense of theatre is of such magnitude that only the Nuremburg rallies or Napoleon's crowning can be compared with the spectacle he put on that night.

His touch of genius was to have dwarves at the ball, giving it an air of decadent extravagance. Laurels were strewn on the floor, with thousands of rose buds and rose heads also serving as carpets. Tumblers and jugglers performed throughout, and the orchestra of course had been flown in from America. I was, as always, the last man to leave. For the next two days I brooded on why the night had been so short. It was like having experienced a masterpiece in the making. But it was more poignant than a masterpiece, because its beauty was evanescent, and gone with the dawn.

Taki, Spectator

Only those closest to the Queen can know the signs. A tiny shudder, visible only to the most observant and knowledgeable of eyes, sends a tremor through her body.

Then her normally lively eyes go blank, with just a hint of dreaded anticipation.

Finally, the extreme corners of her mouth flinch down in an expression of brief misery.

These small imperceptive changes are the Queen's all too human response to those duties which she dreads.

Paul Callan, Daily Mirror

ANTHONY BURGESS

The great William Byrd was, as it were, laterally didactic.

Anthony Burgess, Spectator

His hero, Leopold Bloom, has breakfast and then goes to the lavatory, which is what everybody does. But, before Joyce, writers had been scared of admitting this profound truth.

Anthony Burgess, Radio Times

Dr French prefers, at least at the beginning, gender to sex, in some ways an unfortunate term, since it evokes linguistic accidence – the least dynamic aspect of language and unknown to the tongues of the East – and implies a taxonomy based only metaphorically on the sexes, whereas Dr French means real sexes or, if you wish, literal masculinity and femininity.

Anthony Burgess, Observer

The structural essence of all proverbs is to be found on Page 41 of the Eulenburg score of Richard Strauss's "Don Quixote".

Anthony Burgess, Observer

Lem is the other great Pole of our time, scientist, philosopher, futurologist, novelist, trickster, very different from John Pole. His new book is the first book reviewed in this book of imaginary book reviews. Lem is not-Lem reviewing not-Lem as Lem, or perhaps Lem I enclosing Lem 2, or the other way about. The title of the book means that it is a book 'about nothing'. In that the books reviewed do not, and cannot, exist, the reviews cannot exist either. Nor can my own review exist. Let us pretend that it does.

Anthony Burgess, Observer

What is Rome: a mother or a father? It's not a city of coy architectronic curves;

although the roads are femininely sinuous. The palaces are beautiful, but the elegance is masculine. St. Peter's dome isn't the breast of a supine woman, but a great obscene testicle or the swelling in the throat of a rampant peacock.

Anthony Burgess,
Alitalia Airlines magazine

So let us go on having the trivia of these daily radio programmes – the dog that has learned to smoke a pipe is fussy about his brand of tobacco, the farm labourer who has grown a new set of teeth at 80, the blonde computer operator who has become Miss Ilfracombe.

These, when you come to think of it, are not really trivia at all. Great beauty is a miracle, even if it has to be vulgarised in a seaside contest, and we perhaps need beauty queens more than we need politicians.

A pipe-smoking dog adds nothing to the Gross National Product, but he asserts the capacity of the world for giving us new surprises, thus making it worthwhile to go on living; perhaps tomorrow there will be a snuff-taking panda.

Anthony Burgess, Daily Mail

CANDY

Psychological research has shown that hard-centred chocolate bars like Crunchie tend to be eaten by people who externalise their worries when they are under stress. Soft-centred bars, like Milky Way, however, tend to be chosen by people who can internalise their worries. This seems to bear out Professor E. H. Gombrich's theory that there are two distinct personality types: the "biters" and the "suckers".

Combining, as it does hard and soft characteristics, the Mars bar appeals to both biter and sucker. It is the bar of compromise or consensus. It has all the respectability of a food.

New Society

Sir, – I feel this may be an opportune moment to publish the fact that I am seriously using tubes of Smarties in order to help my patients recognise their oral needs to allay anxiety and to give them a way of communicating with me that they are feeling depressed and worried.

There are many adolescents who are not suffering from endogenous depression but have social problems which burden them and they make an appeal for help by taking a handful of the nearest tablets. But for those young people for whom I prescribe Smarties, two or three times a day and overdoses when required, I am quite sure that this gift from me to them has reduced the number of attempted suicides and the need for ambulance and hospital attention, has enabled group therapy to be more meaningful, and is more valuable than the usual placebo.

My colleagues tease me, but I have found that some social workers have copied the idea, and, when given with concern and care, it can be a valuable adjunct to psychotherapy.

Josephine M. Lomax Simpson
British Medical Journal

ANGELA CARTER

Excretion is his (the child's) first concrete production and, through it, the child gains his first experience of labour relations. He may reserve the right to go on excremental strike or to engage in a form of faecal offensive.

Angela Carter, The Sadeian 'Woman'

Breaking with the Christmas tradition of asking literary figures to nominate the book of the year we asked Angela Carter 'what books are at your bedside?'

'Loom and Spindle or Life Among the Early Mill Girls by Harriet Robinson. Amoskeag (a description of a New England mill town). The Communist Manifesto.'

Quarto, December 1981

. . . it is no wonder that mirrors figure so often in the apparatus of soft-core porn, along with ostrich feathers, mesh stockings, straw hats and other less iconographically gripping sorts of kitsch.

Angela Carter, Vogue

"I once saw a man puking exhaustively inside the Abbey," Carter says, writing about Bath. It's not that the puke – or her mention of the puke – is a protest, and in spite of her title and my remarks on it, Carter is not an iconoclast. She is something more subtle: a libertarian. The puke is a piece of the truth which decorum denies, just as Bath, in Carter's view, *"a city so English that it*

feels like being abroad," conspires to deny the crudities of the present and aims immediately for nostalgia.

Michael Wood, reviewing Angela Carter's "Nothing Sacred" in New Society

COUNTRY LIFE

Kent: It was one of those late autumn days when the landscape looked uncommonly kind and colourful, the butterburr in flower giving a touch of spring. We walked and talked about tints and textures and agreed that the field maple was the finest of them all. Then one of the company commented on the sounds underfoot. She noted that different leaves made different noises. They felt different, too, she said. This stunned us into silence and we engaged in a kind of foot conversation with the leaves. Whitebeam in crisp rolls crunched even more than curled beech. Oak leaves were stiff with spangle galls. Ash fell green and made the softest carpet. It was novel at least and made us feel even more in tune with the day.

John T. White, Guardian

I remember the happiest moment of my life. I was living in Wimbledon Park and it was one of those hot summer days in 1976. I was sitting in the garden and listening to Tchaikovsky's Violin Concerto for the first time, and a bee came and sat on my leg and peed. I didn't know bees could pee. I could feel my eyes filling up with tears and I felt an intense spiritual happiness.

Lesley-Anne Down, Tatler

I lay down in a wet field last week to listen to the sound of sheep grazing. It is not an easy matter. First, the silly creatures bound away. Next they remain rooted at some distance, staring: *not* grazing. But after an hour, their curiosity equalling mine, I was rewarded by the sound of a mute, contented slush counter-pointed by a quiet grinding.

Jacky Gillot, The Listener

We have been out in the soft mists of an East Anglian autumn, in the harsh winds of frosty December, we have seen the pale wash of sunshine in earliest spring. Against this background we have witnessed animals' – horses, hounds and foxes – engaged in a thrilling contest of instinct and skill. We have ridden past old houses rarely seen by strangers, and moved through lonely woods and coverts as through a secret landscape.

In time I came to understand that hunting offers a more active and more intimate experience of the country than does any other sport.

Professor J. P. Stern,
Cambridge Evening News

COUPLES

Yet here she sits warm as a sister, lovely as a swan, as blandly self-assured as ever as she dips unceremoniously into her right eye for a rogue contact lens and smiles upon the former hard man of British journalism as he talks of joy and love and beauty and the wonderful spiritual change she has helped wreak in him, and I find myself hooked and on the end of her white finger along with Bernard and her small glob of optician's plastic. And when Bernard pronounces that he is more and more convinced of the 'importance of the inexplicable', and Arianna warms to the theme of the mystical nature of human change and of its mysteriously contagious quality, it sounds almost prosaic in its reasonableness.

Sally Vincent on Bernard Levin
and Arianna Stassinopoulos, Observer

I often wake up to a surprise – or a laugh. My wife has such interesting and amazing dreams and she insists on telling me about them as soon as she wakes. The other day she said to me: 'I've dreamt that you have given me a waterfall'. I said. 'What?' She said, 'A waterfall – and all I want now is a hill to go with it.' I thought that a beautiful idea – very exciting. I'm wondering what I can do about it.

Sir Peter Parker, Sunday Times Magazine

George (Best) is always portrayed as nothing but a useless, idiotic boor, permanently at the bottle, and it's so unfair. That's not my husband. That's not the man who lies beside me in bed at night and makes me cry at the beauty of the poetry he's written.

Angie Best, Woman's Own

We had a large sitting room overlooking the sea, and we took two different windows, two typewriters, and we banged away. I on 'The French Lieutenant's Woman', and she on 'Charles II'. And it worked quite well. The music of the typewriters . . . sort of mingled and became . . . I don't know . . . not that they became one, but . . .

Harold Pinter, Sunday Times Magazine

At 32, Mike Batt, creator of a whole string of pop hits, upped and left his comfortable home in England to sail the world with his wife and two children. For Wendy Batt the change in lifestyle was something so vast that she decided to go out and have a small Japanese chrysanthemum tattooed on the top of her thigh. "That was for me a way of signalling our new freedom," she says.

Ray Connolly, Sunday Express Magazine

Round about 1a.m. we have a cup of Earl Grey tea in bed. Then we read until we fall asleep. We take several papers. Tom cuts out any items, political, medical, arts, etc, which he knows will interest me and I go through them. Or I read seed catalogues and photography catalogues, or the occasional glossy mag. Then we fall asleep, my right cheek resting on Tom's left shoulder. Always in the same way, knowing the day is over and everything is all right.

Miriam Stoppard, talking to Gail Curtis, Sunday Times Magazine

CRACKERS

We believe that the most important assets of United Biscuits are its brands. Buildings age and become dilapidated. Machines wear out. Cars rust. People die. But what lives on are the brands.

R.C. Clarke, M.D. United Biscuits Saatchi & Saatchi's Annual Report

CRITICS

However, if we look at the relationship established with the pre-existing dimension within which the created object is placed, we become aware of the acceptance of a dialogue which admits the existence of the dialectical pole of an objective horizon and its confrontation, although the perspective of a total redefinition founded upon the inserted object; it will be noted also – as Argan has recently aptly remarked – that the action tends to occur not so much through a forced upheaval of the predetermined structural field or the quantitive demands of the inserted object, as through the emotive force of the new presence, borne over a plane of gentle modulations.

From 'Andrea Palladio' by Lionelli Puppi, translated by Pearl Sanders

Yet we should honour skill where it occurs. There are some attractive and beautifully contrived poems in Mahon's new collection. The best remain mysterious under a surface, mellifluousness. 'A Garage in Co. Cork' develops the desolate vision of his earlier 'A Disused Shed in Co. Wicklow'.

Peter Porter, Observer

To my astonishment, at the age of 40, I am a British peeress (the Lady Vaizey), the mother of three wildly active adolescents, and the art critic of the London Sunday Times. Every Sunday, six million readers will at least glance at what I say.

In the week I travel through Britain, Europe, and occasionally America looking at shows. And then I serve on the Arts Council of Great Britain, which sponsors most music, drama, and art in Britain.

Private and public life intertwine, sometimes leaving little room to breathe. It has family benefits. The children suddenly say, "Oh look, that man's a Magritte!" and used to sign their scribbles "Piccasso" (sic).

Marina Stansky Vaizey, '59 Art critic, peeress
Radcliffe Quarterly

There is a brilliant introduction to the challenging new literature of Santiago Ginsberg, whose aim has been to create a poetic language "made up of terms which have no exact equivalent in common language but which denote

*situations and sentiments that are,
and always were, the essential theme
of the lyric." As Ginsberg has written:
"hloj ud ed pta jabuneh Jrof Grugno."*

Ciaran Carty, Sunday Independent

Julian Barnes is 36 years old. He has the
craggy good looks that would make a
romance writer reach for the word
craggy. There is a little of Punchinello
and still more of St Bruno. His voice is
modulated and deep but, according to
Martin Amis, his humour reaches even
greater depths.

Olinda Adeane, Harpers

Commonsense tends to elide the very
precise difference between the two, so that
margaret drabble shades into Margaret
Drabble. Commonsense, therefore lends
itself to the cult of authorship, in whichever
version. Margaret Drabble as extra-text,
margaret drabble as super-text. In both,
Margaret Drabble stands over and above
margaret drabble as the source, truth and
guarantee of the text. They differ in one

respect: with Margaret Drabble as extra-text, Margaret Drabble as super-text, margaret drabble is ignored, having performed its/her function. This last point is essential: to get into authorial orbit you need the preliminary (dischargable) stage of the text. Margaret Drabble (writer, inhabitant of NW3) becomes Margaret Drabble (author) because of margaret drabble (a set of features characterising her books).

Mike Westlake 'The Artful Reporter'
June '68

Mr Hattersley is the Flaubert of Fleet Street.

Alexander Chancellor, The Listener

ECOLOGY

I'm deeply into shit. It's ridiculous what we do with our waste. I'm doing subtle reading like "Excreta disposal in rural districts" and I'll probably produce a little booklet.

Tony Wigens, 'Vole' Magazine

I suppose I should mention toilets. We use two electric humus-producing toilets, which once a year give us a trayful of rich black geranium-potting material that we package and give to our friends as tokens of esteem.

Stanley Burke, 'The Canadian' Magazine

AMAZON DREAM: Escape to the Unknown
Robert Reed.
Feeling inexplicable hurt and fury about his
perfectly normal upbringing, the author
made a Great Break, when aged 21, and left
home in Kent to live in the Amazon jungle.
His sworn intention was to turn into a tree.
Having become a tree, he would use its
access to natural energy to direct and focus
all Amazon forces into a concerted attack on
Civilization's encroachment on the jungle –
which he believed holy – and then against
civilization in the rest of the world, so
destroying it and bringing about the New
Age.

In Amazon Dream he tells, honestly and
vividly, where he failed and where he
succeeded.

E.O.A. Books, Handout

Tom Merriam is lecturer in environmental studies and English history at Basingstoke Technical College. He was formerly engaged on highway construction and now refuses to own a car.

The Ecologist

ECONOMICS

From its present level the market is just as likely to rise as to fall. To be more precise, the weighted probabilities of movements in either direction are the same. In other words there could be a large chance of a small further recovery or a small chance of a large further drop – or vice versa.

Samuel Brittan, Financial Times

EDUCATION

Humpty-Dumpty sat on a wall,
Humpty-Dumpty had a great fall;
All the King's horses and all the King's men
Couldn't put Humpty together again.   *[Mother Goose]*

Discuss the truth or falseness of the famous poem in light of the second law of thermodynamics.

*Frank C. Andrews –
'Thermodynamics: Principles & Applications'*

Gridsheets provide an open-ended situation. They are the tool of the thinking teacher. The general idea is to provide a framework where the student can create a situation and then offer conjectural hypothesis to starter questions. The class discussion which flows from varied experience is wide and welcome. It gives students a chance to propose an opinion, change their mind, become convinced and even change their mind again to a refined thought. The workbook 'Making Thinking Visible' illustrates the philosophy.

Greater London Council Supplies Department, July 1982

Two last chats for 1977 have been planned for Thursday 15 December at 7.00:
Bob Evans: Empty spaces
Max Boisot: The Cuban missile crisis and its influence on architectural criticism.

Architectural Association Events List

When a teacher canes a child he is indulging not just in a couple of short, sharp blows to the bottom. He is celebrating a kind of ritual mass at the altar of his particular ideals.

Polly Toynbee, Gardian

COGNITIVE CYCLES IN EARLY DEVELOPMENT, Dr Norman Freeman – *University of Bristol*

Infants gain knowledge about the canonical function of cups in the first year of life. This influences their success in search tasks. They largely overcome a canonicality bias in search in the second year of life but it re-emerges in imitation games. After mastering basic imitation, the bias re-emerges. The cycles cannot be attributed to increasing executive complexity of tasks. It is proposed that a basic organising strategy used at one symbolic level is called up when higher symbolic levels are set up. There is some evidence that the contestive status of *in* and *on* does not alter between the imitation and language comprehension levels in 18 month-olds, nor within language over the age-range 18-30 months.

Colloquium Programme,
University of London

ENCOUNTERS

Harold Acton dwells on suggestive syllables, in "Byzantium" the zant is lingered on, accentuated, regretfully discarded while there remains in the mind the faint suggestion of the perfumed East of our imagination.

Or, in "enormous", the norm is emphasized with a rising cadence, the hands extending, seemingly trying to encircle a substance too large to hold.

Lord Lambton, The Times

Virgil Thomson set some of Miss Stein's poems to music, then approached her in Paris for an opera libretto. They decided on the subject of Spanish saints and Miss Stein wrote the text.

"When I read the libretto," Mr Thomson said "I discovered the stage directions were all mixed up with the speeches and with her own reflections about how this is getting on. I thought 'this is rather wonderful' and set the whole thing to music."

Zimbabwe Financial Gazette

Talking to Lester Piggott as he reclines on the sofa at home is like considering an impressionist painting. No bold statements are made, no clear-cut picture at first emerges as you strain forward to catch the muttered, considered phrases. Then gradually light and colour begin to illuminate the canvas of over a quarter of a century of racing history, a period dominated by that slight figure.

Michael Seeley, The Times

'How many ways can a hand hold a rose?'
Professor Salvador Minuchin says softly,
breaking a piece of croissant and putting
it into his mouth. 'Why, so many ways I
would have thought it's unthinkable', say
I. 'No, no, no, no madame,' says
Minuchin, 'it is finite. It depends on the
fingers, on the bones in the hand, in the
arm . . .' and his fingertips dance lightly
up his sleeve. If the system functions
wrongly, throwing up children who are
warped and sick, the whole family has to
be restructured. It is no good
investigating one part of it. He lays his
hand on the table very close to my elbow.
'I do not end where my skin ends,' he
says.

Cynthia Kee, Observer

*When he (Solzhenitsyn) laughed it was as though
laughter were a function of politeness, but never
because he was amused. He went into the
lavatory and when he came out there was a bead
of moisture on the heavy black cloth of his
trouser-leg. I noticed this because, of our
common humanity, it was the single, only thing I
felt any right to claim a share of.*

Robert Robinson in 'The Dog Chairman'

To interview Sylvia Kristel – the original
Emmanuelle – you first have to pick your way
through an assault course thrown up at every
indiscreet turn of phrase by her manager, a
tough New Yorker named Elaine Rich.
  Of Emmanuelle Ms Kristel says: "I have

cried for seven years because of the way
people dismissed it as a porno movie."

"Sylvia was crying inside," intercedes Mrs
Rich. "She was purged for Emmanuelle,
rejected and alone. In the last seven years
she has been raped and pillaged,
conceptually of course. So she thought,
what the hell. Wouldn't you be inclined to
feel a bit wild under those circumstances?"

Clive Ranger, Sunday Times

He [W.H. Auden] kept looking out of the
window and lighting another fag. There was
a tremendous level of pain in him. You
wanted to hold him and remind him of one
of his great inspirational lines: 'Doom is
dark and deeper than any sea dingle'.

Tom Davies, The Observer

*The Keeler residence, an eleventh-
storey council flat in Chelsea, is
uncompromisingly bare, stripped to
the knuckle of austerity. Christine's
two romantic prints, her six tulips,
constitute such tiny concessions to
decoration that they sit like pebbles
beside a sea of deprivation.*

David Leitch, Sunday Times Magazine

I told him about a nun who sat in the back
row of one of my lecture courses and who
one day complained after class that a
couple near her were always spooning.
"Sister", I had said, "in these troubled
times we should be grateful if that's all

they were doing", and related this to Nabokov rather smugly, proud of what I deemed to be my quick wit. *"Ohhh"*, moaned Nabokov, mourning my lost opportunity, clapping his hand to his head in mock anguish, "You should have said, 'Sister, be grateful that they were not forking'."

The brilliance of at least the latter pun reinforces one's sense of that aura of invincibility and absolute authority which Nabokov projected so successfully in his many prefaces, interviews, and letters to the editor (see his *Strong Opinions*).

Alfred Appel Jnr. 'Memories of Nabokov', Times Literary Supplement

There was a nice moment while talking to Kirk Douglas. He has really wild, stary eyes, and was talking about his son's new film when I started studying his famous dimple. It is the original black hole of the film business and, finally, I mustered up the nerve to ask if I could put my finger in it. His jaw shot out. 'Be my guest. It'll bring you luck.' It was exquisite and I got my finger back too.

Pendennis, The Observer

The two-tone Rolls whispers up the drive of the big country mansion hideaway, its fat tyres scrunching the gravel.

The driver steps out, wraithlike in a loose white dress, her hair a rolling sea of deep-red gold on gold. "Hi, I'm Marti Caine."

Inside the house, in the cool gleaming-white lounge that gives out on to lawns, ducks and a deep slow mill stream, she examines you – mentally circling like a dog with a bone that may have been poisoned.

You feel that here is a woman in the prime of her life who has scars to conceal – and heart and guts big enough to drive the QE2.

William Marshall, Daily Mirror

FASHION

Translucently Sheer Pantyhose

The ultimate pantyhose experience. Yves Saint Laurent casts his fashion spell with a new, near-incredible yarn. A yarn so translucently sheer and whisper-light that the pantyhose minify into elfin-shape when in repose. Only when they're on will you appreciate the pure magic of it all. The feeling is indescribably sensuous. Sandalfoot with imperceptible run-resist band.

Packaging – Creative Hosiery Brands Co.

Adventurous people are wearing food already – a marmite sandwich, a carrot earring – others at least considering the idea. Anything can be snatched from a plate or refrigerator and worn with style. Of course it becomes mouldy, it rots, but there is plenty more when you tire of its

pungency. Food stains – the conceptual end of the market – will thrill. For the conventional, gravy and mint sauce on their neckties; egg and trifle will be high street fashion; rare and out of season stains clamoured for by the ultra chic.

Arnolfini Review

FILMS

Why does a man cross the screen carrying a sack early in this movie? Why does the same man, transplanted from Seville to Paris, appear again carrying what seems to be the same sack? Why does Mathieu show up in one scene carrying this sack? Why does he take it with him when he goes out to dinner? Why does it appear in the window of a shop in a Paris arcade? Does it have anything to do with the sack of excrement, already mentioned? I don't think these questions need an answer. What is important is to understand how the possibility of a meaning for this sack *spoils* its gratuitous presence in the film as an *objet trouve (et retrouve).* The very possibility of a meaning ruins a certain form of freedom, and it is this ruin and this freedom which Bunuel wishes us to understand. He offers neither nostalgia nor wisdom, but an engaging practical example of the art of accepting defeat without learning to expect it.

Michael Wood,
New York Review of Books

The film has some almost Chekovian subtleties and an Ibsenite sense of passion while remaining completely Indian.

Derek Malcolm, Sight & Sound

FOOD & DRINK

Elizabeth David dislikes uniformity, as all true cooks do. How right she is to blame the toaster that aspires to produce evenly brown slices. She uses instead a metal plate over the gas burner that makes every piece different, "differently marked, irregularly chequered with the marks of the grill, charred here and there, flecked with brown and gold and black..."

Claire Tomalin, Sunday Times

Bruce Jay Friedman stands in his kitchen, praising a limp piece of veal: "Veal," he says stabbing at the sad specimen with a spatula, "is the quintessential lonely-guy meat.

"There's something pale and lonely about it. Especially if it doesn't have any veins – you know it isn't going to hurt you."

Paul Dacre, Daily Express

Ah, how to describe those cheeses? There was something grave and noble from Burgundy, modulating as it were from the sage gravitas of E flat to the tragedy of G minor; two impudent little goats' milk cheeses full of gamin high spirits, the one stern, almost brutal, the other gaily prancing, a Ray Hankin and a Liam Brady, as it were.

Geoffrey Wheatcroft, Spectator

Eaters of asparagus know the scent it lends the urine. It has been described as reptilian, or as a repulsive inorganic stench, or again as a sharp, womanly odour . . . exciting. Certainly it suggests sexual activity of some kind between exotic creatures, perhaps from a distant land, another planet. This unworldly smell is a matter for poets and I challenge them to face their responsibilities.

Ian McEwan, Boulevard

I wonder, each day, why Wordsworth never wrote a poem to the glories of loaves rather than nature, so luscious are the shades of gold and rust, far more beautiful than leaves, so sensual the shapes; far more so than hills.

Margaret Forster, Punch

A soufflé is always a very special compliment to your guests. It is its ephemeral nature that is responsible for the mystique of the soufflé. Brought to the table straight from a hot oven in the full glory of its lofty architecture, it lasts only for a moment of drama and acclaim. Then it must be eaten at once or it will disappear of its own accord. Thus a sweet excitement climaxes the dinner and, not lasting long enough for reconsideration or ennui, the airy soufflé leaves a more intriguing memory than sturdier fare.

Anna Thomas, The Vegetarian Epicure

Harrogate Sparkle, however, is freshly brisk, with a touch of stimulating impatience, though perhaps a little thin and nervous. It is much less bland and assured than Sparkling Ashbourne (Derbyshire), which is more full-bodied and flat in its personal manner.

Dennis Barker (on Mineral Waters)
Guardian

Baked Beans

CROSSE & BLACKWELL 17½p

COOPER: If you are going to embrace a concept of baked beans in tomato sauce then this is a good example. The smell and taste are pleasant, they look nice and seem as if they would be quite tasty when cold, which is the way some people like to eat baked beans. I enjoyed these.
GRIGSON: A robust, earthy smell. These have more of a vegetable taste, as if what was in them once actually grew – a rewarding experience in a tinned

product. You get a beany texture which is quite separate from the sauce.

MOSIMANN: Very pleasant taste. The texture is nicely cooked – the beans don't stick together like in other brands.

WINFIELD (Woolworth) 18½p

COOPER: Very, very good. It's runnier than most, a higher proportion of sauce to beans. I cannot help feeling this is the bean I have been eating all my life. Woolworth's? I'm going to go out and buy some of these.

GRIGSON: Really a good bean. I prefer the slightly earthy taste of the one we had earlier but not to any great extent. Good flavour, good smell, good texture. And the vinegar adds a little intensity.

MOSIMANN: This appeals just a bit more than the others. There is a happiness about these beans, the colour is fresh and alive. Ah, the vinegar. That accounts for the shininess of the individual bean.

Observer Colour Magazine

GAMES

You don't have to be an art critic to step into the Louvre in Paris and know instantly you are in the presence of genius.

Comparing Leonard with the Old Masters may be considered a grossly exaggerated analogy.

But watching him at work with his palette of princely punches has convinced me he has been blessed with a God-given talent.

I don't mind admitting I've regarded boxing at its highest level as an art form.

Colin Hart, The Sun

The difference between United and Arsenal for me can be likened to the inexplicable difference between Wizard and Hotspur, The 39 Steps and Swallows and Amazons, Marilyn and Liz Taylor, Graveney and Barrington, Lucinda and Princess Anne, Terry Wogan and Bruce Forsyth, Randall and Greig, Reggie Bosanquet and Alistair Burnett. I have honestly never had a close friend who supported Arsenal.

Frank Keating, Guardian

Football on television is glamorous, a game of chess at 30 m.p.h. in which bouffant combatants dance minuets of delicious skill between each other's swirling feet. It is a tournament of liveried poppin-jays enacted before hordes of sturdy yeoman fans.

Ray Connolly, Standard

Pratt got one back for Spurs with a deflected shot off Needham, and Spurs, scenting survival at 1-2, controversially substituted the powerful Villa for the creative Ardiles. It failed to work. Instead, with time running out O'Hare put Birtles

*through for Forest's third goal. That
left us to contemplate Plato's
observation that beauty is simplicity.*

Geoffrey Green, The Times

When, in 1971, India took the first-
innings lead against England at Lord's
for only the second time ever in this
country, Indian journalists distributed
sweets to mark the occasion. It was
difficult not to believe that it was a
moment of great religious significance.

Mihir Bose, Sunday Times

*The notorious example is Old, a wonderfully
subtle bowler on his rare day, but a man who
finds it regrettably difficult to keep muscle, bone,
nerve and sinew in the wondrous patterns laid
down by their maker. Hendrick, were he truly to
explode in the delivery stride, would buckle those
giant hinges at once; and as for Willis . . . he is
really the wonder of the age, because his
consistent success is achieved only after he has
fought his arhythmic nature to submission, time
after time, all the way to the crease.*

Russell Davies, New Statesman

Tennis is the most purely formal sport, an oddly Anglo Saxon mixture of creativity and masochism with some of the peripheral characteristics of drama thrown in.

Catherine Bell, Tennis Magazine

William Hartson, a chess master himself, offered a fine blend of art and artlessness. "This is a bad bishop", he would remark. "Of course it is a good bishop in this position, but it has an existential quality of badness. It's a good bad bishop.

David Spanier, The Times

The shot of the week was the first red in the 135 break which finally took Higgins triumphantly to the title.

Forty shades of grey flickered around his urban urchin eyes, skin like dappled putty and features creased like a crumpled bookie's docket as he tensed, terrified at the daring of what he was about to attempt before hitting the white ball so hard that had it been a cricket ball he'd have skewered in cleanly on the cue, sent it funnelling fiercely down the table to fire the red into the corner and stop dead as a gloved fist thumped in a wall, precisely, inched perfectly on the black.

Eamonn McCann, Socialist Worker

The art of snooker is not the mere potting of reds and colours; it is the fastidious control of the white ball position after the stroke has been completed.

But the worst crime of all was the utter lack of sensibility in giving us a dehydrated 'highlight' version of Mr Spencer's beautiful break of 138, as if a sonnet could be shortened by printing the line-endings. Breaks like Spencer's and Reardon's are not amassed; they are composed or created and have the fleeting beauty of a song by Kathleen Ferrier. If we can't have the whole, or an intelligible quotation, then let us have none of it.

James Phoenix, Letters–Radio Times

GEOPOLITICS

Sir, – Why should all the globes and maps of the world be made with North at the top? The world is in space.

So let us declare a moratorium on "North at the top" for a number of years. "North at the top" means, mostly, whites at the top. Down with racialist maps, I say. Bottoms up for a change.

Donald Bissett, Guardian Letters Page

INTUITION

There is a feeling that all broadcasters get once in a lifetime. You are sitting in a studio, the lights are dim, perhaps a lone lamp. Suddenly, because of some psychic force, you are broadcasting to nobody at all. Nobody anywhere is listening. And, because of this, words over which you have worked travel away and beyond the human consciousness, up into a place where dimensions you know nothing about take them over and store them up.

Frank Delaney, The Listener

JONATHAN MILLER

Jonathan Miller demanded that I should come and live with him during rehearsals. 'You're coming home with me and from today you'll live like a monk,' he said. 'You're not going to read a paper, watch television, you're going to live in my son's room until this thing is over.' He literally took me over. Magic. I'd be working on the script, come downstairs with a thought and he'd cross reference it with a monk in the 14th century.

Bob Hoskins, 'Over 21'

A life-size picture of Goethe, the bleached skeletons of a chicken and frog, a Sudanese distilling pot, a set of Hogarth etchings and all the books ever written on Mesmer and animal magnetism – these are some of the things that immediately greet the visitor to Jonathan Miller's house in Regent's Park, London, a fair illustration of his magnetic personality.

Radio Times

Every collection of books gives an index to the character of the collector. Jonathan Miller's books go further. He can show that the arrangement of titles on his wall of shelves makes, in itself, "a proposition about the nature of knowledge": to him it represents "an objective correlate" to the workings of his mind; and he sees that one set of books on the subject standing against another set on another subject gives weight to his feelings for "the seamlessness of knowledge".

Neil Lyndon, Sunday Telegraph Magazine

THE WORLD OF LEARNING

Normally reading is an audio-visual verbal processing skill of symbolic reasoning, sustained by the interfacilitation of an intricate hierarchy of sub-strata factors that have been mobilised as a psychological working system and pressed into service in

accordance with the purpose of the reader.

Dr. Ellen O'Leary, Irish Times

Personal Space Invasions in the Lavatory

R. Dennis Middlemist et al. (Oklahoma State Univ.) in *Journal Personality & Social Psychology* 33:541-6, May 76 [pd 2918b]

... The authors describe an experiment in which 60 users of men's lavatory at a US university were observed while urinating in three conditions: alone, adjacent to a confederate, or at a distance from a confederate. An observer stationed in a toilet stall used a periscope apparatus to view the subject's "lower torso" and timed the "delay and persistence of micturition" using two stopwatches. Subjects were "not informed that they had participated in an experiment". The authors conclude that "close interpersonal distances increased the delay of onset and decreased the persistence of micturition. These findings provide objective evidence that personal space invasions produce physiological changes associated with arousal".

Current Contents

The publication of a new volume of the Cambridge Economic History is itself an historical event. Like a great freight train, bursting out from its dark tunnel, it rattles across our landscape, loaded high with gold and spices, coal and lumber – a few peasants, merchants,

silk-hatted bankers, officials, the businessmen clinging to the roofs of the cars. Livestock are terrified and students astonished; but as happy economic historians we line the tracks and wave our greetings, and then as the noise and smoke fade away, we return to our firesides to tell each other stories of what we have seen.

This time it is Volume VI, The Industrial Revolutions and After, that has gone by.

Journal of Economic History

JOHN SPARROW ON. . .

'If you do put your empty cigarette packet into the bin, then it isn't litter. The legend must surely mean "for what would (or might) be litter if you don't put it in here".'

The retired Warden of All Souls College, Oxford, reflects on *Public notices.*

(Repeat)

Radio Times

We examined the effects of the closures of 10 branch lines in different parts of the country between 1969 and 1976. We found that the closures have brought about a marked diminution of former rail-based activities among a significant proportion of the local population.

Policy Studies Institute Letter to The Times

This journal aims at enhancing the nascent dialogue on the level of rhetoric as well as that of fundamental synthesis. It will play a unifying role,

*in providing a common means of
publication for those in widely
differing disciplines who, directly or
indirectly, are contributing to the
structural aspects of the phenomena
exhibited in human social systems.*

Journal of Social and Biological Structures

*Pumple is the English puppallemaasa, which
excited me, but the OED is very scathing about
people who imagine that this is the original word
for grapefruit, rather than a South Indian
corruption of the Dutch word of which the first
half probably means pumpkin, while the second
half is the Dutch transcription of the Old
Javanese distortion of the Portuguese version of
"lemon" (but you probably knew that).*

Eric Korn, Times Literary Supplement

BERNARD LEVIN

The Taj Mahal seems to be made of air, and
the effect it had on me was to induce a kind of
cosmic sadness, which grew in intensity
through the hours I spend there every day (I
stayed three days in the vicinity), until I
began to feel it would kill me; on the last
evening, when I turned to leave, with no
more time in hand than was necessary to get
to the airport, I did not dare to look back
through the arch at the framed view as I left,
for the fear of being turned into a pillar of
marble and for the certainty that I would weep.

This laceration of the heart I also feel when I hear the main theme of the adagio of the Ninth Symphony, when I stand before one of the late Rembrandt self-portraits, and every time I go down the Grand Canal.

Bernard Levin, The Times

I love Mozart: I revere Beethoven; I am humbly uncomprehending before Bach; I revel in Verdi; I wallow in Richard Strauss; I enjoy Rossini; I don't care much for Tchaikovsky; I dislike Mahler; I am bored by Berlioz. But all these feelings about all these composers are on a human scale; all of them, even Beethoven – even Mozart – produce in me emotions, the dimensions of which I can measure, the origins of which I can see, and the effect of which I can control. But Wagner demands of me, as he demands of everyone, total surrender, the absolute abnegation of self, the complete absorption in his genius of my heart, my mind, my very soul.

Bernard Levin, TV & Entertainment Times (Hong Kong)

Levin's sentences are, of course, something else again. One is drawn as if into the Doges' palace in Venice, enticed by a fresco at the end of a subordinate clause, taken deeper into vast twilit chambers by an adroit semi-colon, sustained down echoing conjunctive corridors by the distant gleam of a conclusion. Every reader going into a Levin column should have a pocketfull of his own full stops.

Harold Evans, Sunday Times reviewing 'Taking Sides' by Bernard Levin.

Amid the din of special pleading for special interests, the thunderbus rustle of wool being pulled over eyes, and the rattle of skeletons being hastily thrust back into closets, Private Eye's savage sanity provides a just counterpart to the swineries in public life.

Bernard Levin, Sunday Times Magazine

But to this day, also, I cannot hear Bach's Third Brandenburg Concerto without conjuring up the magical years in which I was making my journey into music. We cannot remember how the practice began but . . . provided the perfect coda for such occasions, and left us hungry for more when the next occasion presented itself. I later heard it played, with variations, by a busking violinist in a passageway of the Madrid underground, and the trick worked instantly; before three bars had gone by, I was drowning in memories.

Bernard Levin, The Times

Bhagwan Shree Rajneesh

I came away, impressed, moved, fascinated, by my experience of this man (or God, or conduit, or reminder) and the people ("be ordinary and you will become extraordinary") around him. I came away, also, to a haunting fragment of time; beside the road leading to the ashram there was, in addition to the beggars, a pedlar selling simple wooden flutes. As I passed him for the last time he was playing a familiar tune: how he had learnt it, and what he believed it to be, I could not even begin to imagine. It was "Polly put the kettle on".

Bernard Levin, The Times

MARX

At the risk of seeming facetious, I think it fair to say that Marx would have been rivetted by motorcycle racing.

Barry Coleman, New Manchester Review

Loud laughter at dinner softens as the night proceeds into murmurs. Voices drop. In the moonlight, one of us at table, a young man but from an old, wily culture, lists the three essentials of life: the security of the house; war and manliness; the pleasures of the bed. You realise at once where Marx went wrong.

Edward Mace, The Observer

From each according to his abilities, to each according to his needs – the great Communist proposition expounded by Karl Marx needs very little alteration before it can be applied perfectly to the egalitarianism of four-wheel-drive.

LK Setright, Car

MEDICINE

Few who reach middle age can claim never to have had any symptoms related to the anus. Thomson has shown elegantly, if not originally, that what many regard as piles are normal vascular cushions. We all have them, and they are as natural as the vascular cushions at the upper end of the alimentary tract that we call lips. We are prepared to accept a wide variety of lips; and even hot lips. Similarly, variations in the vascular cushions at the anus should possibly be regarded as signs of character rather than disease.

J. Alexander-Williams,
British Medical Journal

SCROTAL ASYMMETRY AND RODIN'S DYSLEXIA.

McManus has pointed out that most artists depict the left testicle of man lower than the right, in accordance with the facts. An exception occurs in Rodin's famous sculpture L'Age d'Airan where the right testicle of the figure seems (from photographs we have seen) to hang lower than the left. We should like to suggest that Rodin was genuinely confused about left and right.

M. J. Morgan, Nature

He has been described in the medical press as the man who "has given status to flatus and class to gas". Indeed, Dr Michael Levitt, a gastroenterologist from Minneapolis, Minnesota, has made the study of intestinal gas his life's work. He has been able to provide answers to such pressing questions as what causes gas,

*how much gas a person normally
passes and why stools float. Nothing
like it has been done before.*

Macleans Magazine (Canada)

Hair, like skin, is a "natural" part of the
surface of the body, but unlike skin it
continually grows outward, erupting
from the body into the social space
beyond it. Inside the body, beneath the
skin, it is alive and growing; outside,
beyond the skin, it is dead and without
sensation, although its growth manifests
the unsocialised biological forces within.
The hair of the head thus focuses the
dynamic and unstable quality of the
frontier between the "natural",
biolibidinous forces of the inner body
and the external sphere of social
relations. In this context, hair offers itself
as a symbol of the libidinal energies of the
self and of the never-ending struggle to
constrain within acceptable forms their
eruptions into social space.

Dr. Terence Turner, New Scientist

MUSIC

Verse for Sibelius Kullervo Symphony:
'Come into my sledge, O maiden,
Underneath my rug, my dearest,
And you there shall eat my apples,
And shall crack my nuts in comfort.'

Gerald Larner,
Scottish National Orchestra programme note

The world needs the minimalism of The
Ramones.

It needs a band who've distilled all
moral, political and social philosophy
down to the phrase "gabba gabba hey" –
and it needs it now.

Yeah.

Mick Farren, New Musical Express

Very tightly orchestrated throughout, it began
quietly and built to a sustained tenseness,
dropping into a peaceful central portion evocative
of falling water on a windy night. It then trailed a
slow circle back to the opening motif, ending on
the hypnotic resonance of a water-filled copper
bowl around whose rim Dnu rubbed a stick. One
was reluctant to hear it die away. A very effective
piece.

Bangkok Post

Wire are not "a good band". Wire are not "a
bad band".

Wire are a twist of nylon in a smoke-signal.

Valerie Gaywood, New Musical Express

MALCOLM ARNOLD

Arnold's profundity usually manifests itself in pseudo-shallowness, which is his historical inversion of pseudo-depth.

Hans Keller, Radio Times

I envisage music as a centre of gravity around which all forms of cultural and intellectual experience are gathered and re-formulated in terms of critical subjective perception. Form in music is thus analogous to a grid through which the productive and reproductive prehistory of individual work and genre may be actively incorporated and ideologically re-evaluated as integral components of the expressive discourse itself. Composition is the result of the violent collision of undifferentiated creative volition and such strategically dispositioned mechanisms.

Brian Ferneyhough,
Peters Edition Contemporary Music Catalogue

Professor Thuarwaechter's piano concert at Hotel Meridien, Abu Dhabi, on Thursday evening, held the audience spell-bound for about two hours. Playing selections from Mozart, Beethoven, Ravel and Chopin, the famous pianist conjured up magically reverberant visions of piercingly overwrought spirits juxtaposed with soft and poignant shapes.

Khaleej Times

PERSONAL

Can an intelligent lady, up to late thirties or thereabouts perhaps, alone, attractive, not tall, knowing or having known heartbreak, yet sensitive, warm, humorous, gentle, an aesthete, music-loving, caring for pets and plants, feel sufficient curiosity to write and exchange photographs or telephone a reciprocal male, late fifties, fit, vigorous, working (but with ideas for escaping into clean air) and searching for contributive

anodyne for sudden loss? Mutuality sought in caring, humour, partnership, listening, counselling, learning. Some interests offered include the musical, literary and poetic (passive and creative), reading and being read to, travel, exploration of mountains and mankind, country crafts, nutrition, baking Lucullian bread, small is beautiful, opera, Wagner, Britten, Brahms, Ligetti, Whitman, Cummings – and her own preferences, the search for stillness in one with a reverence for life and yet fire in the belly.

Time Out

Gentle is the light that helps me see, and the night that takes her from me, gentle is the girl who breaks my heart, who loves to hurt, who hurts to love, who lives to laugh, who cries to live, who gives me something I don't know, who takes me gently, when she will, and goes. Guy, 27, desires sincere girl for loving relationship.

Time Out

Male Wanted to share comfortable house Kingsbury with three others (two females one male). Garden, c/h, telephone o/r £20 per week. We are searching for a person who has, as we do, a desire for personal growth and awareness, and who believes that a way to achieve this is through openly sharing their feelings in relationships and being prepared to constantly confront, and be confronted with regard to motivation and emotional integrity.

Time Out

PHILOSOPHY AND RELIGION

The golfer is a potent symbol of mortality in contemporary Christian verse.

John Bayley, The Observer

For the last twenty years – intellectually – Jean-Paul Sartre had been my bread and butter, an illustrious name to conjure with, a talisman to touch in hours of intellectual and emotional need, the voice among all others that I could instantly spot and trust. Hardly a day went by but I found myself thinking a Sartrian thought, turning over a Sartrian proposition, thinking of Sartre.

Tommy Murtagh, 'Hibernia'

'Ya', the dishevelled punks in the audience yelled back. 'We want to go to Salvador'. The leader replied: 'Ya'. Crudely lettered signs above the bandstand read: FAG GAY HOMOLEZBO.

'They read Hobbes, not Rousseau' the producer yelled into my ear. I could barely hear him above the din, but for the first time since coming to Los Angeles I felt reassured that western culture had not entirely lost its edge.

Tom Bethell, The Spectator

Man is albuminoid, proteinaceous, laked pearl; woman is yolky, ovoid, rich. Both are exuberant body growths.

Richard Selzer, Current Contents

Since Father Raynes's death in 1960, Nicholas Mosley has abandoned formal and organised Christian thought; nevertheless his novels still engender the mood of religious optimism, and his characters still ask questions about God:

'Do you know this story? Once upon a time there were two trappers in a hut all winter in Alaska. They made an arrangement whereby one of them should do the cooking until the other one found the food too disgusting, then the other would take over. Well, one had been cooking for a very long time and had got fed up because the other one never complained: so he thought he would serve up something truly terrible. So he made a pie out of moose turds. Well, the other one sat in front of the pie and took a mouthful: for a moment he almost spat: then he said, "Moose turd pie! But good!" So the first one had to go on cooking.

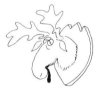

'I think this is a story about God and Man.'

Harper's & Queen

Nozick defines 'auming' as 'what that which is beyond existence and non-existence does'. He says that 'if the only way to knowing what is beyond existence and non-existence and about auming is through an experience of it', then it is possible that 'there is no room for the question "why does it aum?"'

Richard Rorty, 'Persuasive Philosophy'
London Review of Books

*I'm a very emotional thinker. And when I need to
sort myself out – arm myself with good sound
arguments – the New Statesman provides my
spear, my arrows. It's the chariot for my fire.*

Colin Welland, Ad. for New Statesman

There is a small incident in Quiet Days in
Clichy in which Miller, down and out and
hungry but still happy, retrieves the last crust
of bread from the pail, wipes his backside
with it and then eats it. Disgusting though it
may be when read literally, symbolically it is
the gesture of a man who having reached the
lowest point of his existence, has also
managed to reject the models of behaviour
prepared for him by society. For him this is
the point at which liberation begins:
liberation from taboo, from norms and
values, and therefore from guilt and fear of
and for himself.

James Campbell, New Statesman

For most people, life without a newspaper
would be like music without time – a blur of
inchoate sounds, an endless and
incomprehensible cacophony. It is
newspapers which punctuate the march of
time, syncopating their narrative of events
with commentary, analysis and
entertainment. Newspapers comprehend
the sound of history in the making, and give
it meaning.

Times 2nd leader

If you want to be perfect, your search for the naked truth has to rest for the duration of your preoccupation with perfection.

Hans Keller, Spectator

POETRY

When lips sow tender, popping pips, and white
Downy downs shoo-shoo like stroked velvet,
Then magic hills sidle and press, merge
And milk a common root, a gland, a tap,
A loving, ever-suckling source of sweet juice,
And burgeon, blossom, blow a catherine wheel,
Their anthem, their tossed fruits, skyward,
Which – spinning, singing, falling, random,
Whimsical, exact, plum in the middle,
Parachuting peace-boys, bull's-eyeing seed
    bullets –
Tease the silly world with airy Whispers and soft
landings.

Bill Homewood, Country Life

The poem emerges with the quality of observations left to percolate on the back burner of the poet's imagination, where, steeped in his skill, they have slid, inevitably Hobbesian, into their own state of decay.

Michael Carlson,
Reviewing James Fenton's poems

Before Birds Sing

The darkness of night is
  far from the living
    as granite
5:00 am. November

On the panes
  minus fifteen grows
    flowers of ice
5:00 am. December

The morning stove is dead and
  silent as the wood
    of the frozen trees
5:00 am. January

On waking sleep solicits
  another visit
    to her summers
5:00 am. February

Declining he farts
  lights the fire and goes out
    with his churn
5:30 am.

John Berger, New Statesman

*For however many kumquats that I eat I'm not
sure if it's flesh or rind that's sweet, and being a
man of doubt at life's mid-way I'd offer Keats
some kumquats and I'd say: You'll find that one
part's sweet and one part's tart:
Say where the sweetness or the sourness start.*

This single poem should be sufficient
to convince any fair-minded reader that
Tony Harrison's is a most considerable
talent.

Robert Nye, Times

These esoteric parlours of sensibility would
seem opposite in quality to Tom Leonard's
native Glasgow and yet the startling
accuracy with which Leonard transcribes
Glaswegian speech and the smouldering
drunken irony of his poems invite Williams
and Meyer as his most probable
champions. This, for instance:

> "aye
> Moanz aw thi time noo
> stucknthi hooss
>   tied tay thi wainz
> unfulfillt
>
> no lik me thoa
>   bagza overtime
> page three tay wank owr
>   weekend nthi boozirz
> smashd ootma mind
>
> happy iz larry
>   fulfillt iz fuck"

Leonard's poetry carries a class anger that
washes all pretence of colour out of didactic
Marxist verse with which it might be
compared.

Guardian Arts Page

*C'mon said the pilot and the three of us climbed
onto the wing and into the snug plane.
With a short run we took off, lurched upward,
missed a tree top, and found altitude.*

Phew, under your breath. The clipped
excitement is infectious. The title, too, is
laconically clipped (the poem "A Small
Plane in Kansas", or "The . . ."); and them

70

"C'mon" at once gets cracking with its slurred sober casualness. Then there is the precariousness of "and" and "onto" at the ends of the first lines; the pause before take-off, with the full-stop after "plane", on the runway of its line; the feeling in the small of your back from the pressure at the start of the line in "lurched upward".

Christopher Ricks on Thom Gunn, Sunday Times

UNTITLED

Indolently she wept,
Engulfed in the mediocrity of depression.
Spectral birds copulated on the slag heap.
All was silent.
The vocal was complete.
The ant fell from her armpit;
She understood.

*Cathrine Crasspender,
Sussex University Arts Review*

O Britain
Nowhere does a morning dew preserve a
greenness more.
Nowhere do young voices sing as sweet.
O Britain.

O fish & chips.
O dartboard.
And the dark, hopeful corner of a pub.
Ringoland, Paul and John and George's place.
Where Churchill flicked Havana ash.
Lawrence of Arabia rode his motorcycle here, alas.
In summer we fly here, eagerly, caringly, up to 30 times a week.
Come with us.

POLITICIANS

When I saw Guevara's body in the van, he had green socks on his feet and, as I wrote in a dispatch to the Guardian that night, "he wore moccasins as though he had been shot down while running fleet-footed through the jungle."

Yet some years later in Havana, I found myself talking to the Uruguayan writer Carlos Maria Gutierrez, who was then writing the offical Cuban-authorised biography of Guevara. Gutierrez showed me a photograph, which I have never seen reproduced before or since, of Guevara lying apparently dead on a stretcher, but wearing no shoes at all.

By the long shadows on the picture, it looked as though it had been taken in La Higuera in the late evening. In which case, was he already dead on Sunday night, and not shot on Monday? Why were his boots off in the Havana picture, and why was he wearing home-made moccasins when he was displayed in Vallegrande?

For me, it is an unresolved enigma.

Richard Gott, The Guardian

MALCOLM BRUCE – your cycling, cat loving, vegetarian, anti-nuclear, brown rich eating, sandal wearing, wood stove burning, real ale drinking, Scottish Ecology Party candidate for Newtown/Stockbridge.

Election Address

When asked what sight has enthralled him most Mr Pym, the new Foreign Secretary, dismisses from his thoughts the spectacle of 21 years in the Commons, and instead waxes rapturous on a celery picking machine he once saw in the Fens.

His description of the device might appear a mark of a limited outlook, but in practice it stems from a central feature of his art: an ability to deal with most subjects in non-controversial terms.

Nicholas Comfort, Daily Telegraph

We are not just another minor party. We are a unique experience.

Dr. David Owen, Evening Standard

The re-possesion of South Georgia was a wonderful operation. I had the winter at the back of my mind. The winter. What will the winter do? The wind, the cold. Down in South Georgia the ice, what will it do? It beat Napoleon at Moscow.

Margaret Thatcher
talks to George Gale, Daily Express

The Cold War was the product of particular contingencies at the end of world war two, which struck the flowing rivers of political culture into glaciated stasis, and struck intellectual culture with an ideological permafrost.

E.P. Thompson, Guardian

Liz Noonan is the independent lesbian feminist candidate for Dublin South-East.

She introduced me to her friend, advisor and lover, Ruth Jacob, who is assisting her in her campaign. Both

women wore gold wedding bands. Liz
Noonan is deeply committed, deeply
sincere and seems rather saddened by
life.

Dublin Magazine

*Comrades, I had a friend come round tonight,
scared and distraught from the threat of an angry
husband.' He was a gardener, sent for only two
jobs in over two years of unemployment.*

*He seems to have reached the end of his tether
and has spent the day beating her up and scaring
their three young children. What do I do with her
– this strong and beautiful woman?*

*I gave her some wine, some coffee, a cigarette,
and a cuddle. I told her some things Trotsky said,
I told her of our fight for a better life for all – not
just women. And she just cried tears of despair,
listening, but not believing.*

*In the end I was reduced to phoning the
Samaritans for her and settling her for a talk with
them – feeling my inadequacy sharply.*

*Comrades, tell me, I understand the theory –
but tell me, how do I tackle the practical when it
confronts me, in all its horror, on the doorstep at
10.30 p.m. on a Wednesday night?*

M. Pracey, Militant

POMPES FUNÈBRES

So a reader wanted to know what to do with old smoking pipes? Having smoked a series of faithful briars over the past thirty-eight years, I find it very difficult to part with them, but this is what I do.

Removing the worn stem, I give the bowl one last polish on the side of my nose and then drop it into a hole in the front garden.

I've been doing this for years and year after year when doing winter gardening or just forking around the roses in the spring, I often dig one up.

Cleaning off the soil I gently fondle it, remembering summer evenings and long-gone trout-fishing sessions we had spent together. Then I pop it back into the ground for another year.

Eddie Edwards, Letter in Daily Mirror

PORNOGRAPHY

There is a new smell abroad; it is the smell of pornography. It is a real smell, a genuine new odour: acrid, faintly chemical, a snuffed-candle smell, a headache smell.

Martin Amis, The Sunday Times

Prof. James Kinsley, head of the English Department at Nottingham

University, who is also a priest, told the court that the word bollocks was not indecent. He said he had traced it back to Anglo-Saxon times when it meant a small ball. The term was also used to decribe an orchid.

Daily Telegraph

Switchback looks at first like just another piece of badly-written comic pornography, until you realise that Molly Parkin has outdone Robbe-Grillet, undermining traditional assumptions not about art and reality, but about the structure of language itself. It's a stealthy, subversive process that could easily be mistaken for mere carelessness – words missing here and there, confusions of grammar, especially between singular and plural, a dense coating of cliches, and so on. Then suddenly, these devices come together in one bold anti-sentence: 'she viewed herself with the lack of vanity to any professional whose appearance is part and parcel of their work.' It's a stylistic coup that comes soon after what at the time seems no more than a misprint – the world midmight – but is revealed by the ensuing intricacies as a richly ambiguous coinage, with all its tentativeness and moderation, its hypothetical intermediacy . . .

This anti-grammar is the negative

pre-requisite of a more positive achievement, which Parkin shares with Erica Jong: the replacement of outworn grammatical structures with a new sexual rhetoric. In Switchback, as in Parkin's and Jong's other fiction, narratio itself has become a series of sexual positions, and fellatio and cunnilingus are rhetorical tricks.

Jeremy Treglown, New Statesman

The artlessness of her art, and her recurring wryness, are Edna O'Brien's strengths. Nora recalls an ex-lover "getting his tongue sweetly inside the edging of my lovely or unlovely gusset and reinstating the sweetness, the moistures of other times". The choice of the word "gusset" – lovely or unlovely – is extraordinary; the fleeting final insight into the long associations of pleasure is subtle.

*Victoria Glendinning,
Times Literary Supplement*

RELICS

It knocked the bloom off me to watch that silver-framed rose, which Garbo kissed, being sold, along with the rest of Sir Cecil Beaton's belongings.

There lay flushed and eager youth. Blossoming desire. The thorns of passion. All knocked down, in seconds, for £750. When the hammer fell, I never felt so short-lived, and about to crumble into dust.

Jean Rook, Daily Express

SEX

Copulation is undoubtedly man's most animal act. Even as he eats or defecates his mind can be elsewhere, but in copulation body and soul are concentrated in his loins.

Orgasm is the surrogate ectasy peddled by the Devil – an easy pastiche of that mystical state achieved by the most holy saints and ascetics.

Piers Paul Read, The Times

Every sexual act has the potential of affirming the shared past by expressing thanksgiving and gratitude and the mobilization of hope for the future.

Dr Jack Dominian, The Times

I was once alone with a Modigliani nude. She was life-size and lying on a blue cushion in a quiet London gallery. He eyes, typically Modigliani, were dark almonds and her full lips red as strawberries. Everything about her excited me. Her silent, ageless and eternally submissive body caused me to shed my inhibitions. I leaned forward and kissed her between her thighs. It was an exquisite moment.

Somehow it seemed as though painter, model and me became one entity. For that second we were locked in a timeless orgasm, not centred, as it is in the male, in the genitals, but lifted up and placed in a hitherto uncharted region of sexual experience.

Barry Fantoni, Cosmopolitan

While making love to a woman, you are really making love to existence itself.

Bhagwan Shree Rajneesh

Exploring lesbian Sexuality in Dance: Exploring our patterns of lesbian identity, finding and reclaiming our language, giving ourselves nourishment, allowing our body-spirit a safe warm atmosphere and an open time to weave our 'herstory'.

Women's Dance: Going further into our identities as women, how we have been shaped and do shape our own lives. Giving ourselves

time to go deeply and lightly exploring the colours
of our 'female-rainbow-spanning' and the roots
in our body.

Natural Dance Association

STARS

Cometh the hour, cometh the man. There are times in your life when you realise you are dealing with a person who transcends all human limits, and human awareness.

Call him a nutcase, call him a genius, call him what you will, but Brian Clough is one of these men.

Peter Batt, Daily Star

As we consider the recent startling political and journalistic career of Mr Paul Johnson, an image which may spring irresistibly to mind is that of a river crossing a great waterfall. Such a familiar fluminous proceeding may be said to go through three distinct stages. The first, as the distant cataract approaches, is that in which the whole flow of the river seems mysteriously to develop a new, purposeful energy. The current appears to speed up, the surface becomes increasingly flecked with angry eddies to the point where the river even seems at times to be fighting against itself. Then comes the great moment of release when, with a great roar, the torrent moves all at once from one level to another quite different. The third stage, immediately following the change, is that where the river is left boiling in a great maelstrom of froth – from which eventually, one hopes, it recovers, to resume a much more placid and reflective course towards the sea.

Christopher Booker, Spectator

Driberg's autobiography is itself a porridge of glass, in which the splinters of homosexual anguish have been somehow crushed into the consistency of anecdotal muesli.

"Granta '76", (Cambridge University)

THEATRE

The question can there be a Christian novel is like the question whether Shakespeare is Christian, to which the answer is both "profoundly" and "not at all".

Peter Levi, The Times

The plays of Kroetz, who worked as an actor in Fassbinder's Munich anti-theater, have an affinity with Edward Bond's early work: the inarticulacy of the characters in Stallerhof (produced 1971) makes it impossible for them to find out what their problems are, let alone help each other to solve them. Emulating the graceless baldness of journalese, the play presents four introverts on an isolated farm, where the farmer's retarded daughter is impregnated by a labourer who habitually masturbates on the lavatory. The play ends on a note of guarded optimism as the

*farmer's wife, armed with a hosepipe and a
bucket of soapy water, is about to force the metal
nozzle into the girl, who is lying naked on the
kitchen table. Changing her mind, the woman
uses the soapy water to clean the floor.*

Ronald Hayman, Encounter

**A brief mention of the brilliant set by
Eileen Diss, which has more doors than I
have seen on a stage since Adam Pollock's
set for L'Ajo nell' Imbarazzo at Wexford.**

Geoffrey Wheatcroft, Spectator

In another cutting, from the Observer,
Tynan tells of "a septuagenarian
American comic" who being
congratulated on his vitality, said:
"Vitality? I'm so old that I have to
masturbate every morning in order to
start my heart beating."

I wish I had met Tynan. I have been
meaning to ask him who was the author
of this remark.

James Fenton, Sunday Times

*When I look back on 1978 it will not be
Callaghan's face that I shall want to
remember; the bleak logistics of his
world will evoke very little to me, I am
sure. Instead, I shall perhaps
remember a tramp stretched across
three seats in the warm, on the
Victoria line, fast asleep, his right
hand gently cradling his cock, while
the rest of us in the carriage stared*

impassively ahead. What historical forces drew him there? What armies fought? What families fell apart? What compensating impulse guides his hand?

David Hare – Publicity Hand-out for 'Licking Hitler'

"The Dog Beneath The Skin" is a wilful and defiant pageant set against the malignant girders which support the ever so thin veneer of the 1930s chic, and "The sterile proof of summer's perfect fraud".

Press release Half Moon Theatre

TRAVEL

When the A9 road leaves Perth to head northwards in search of Inverness, it takes a journey into schizophrenia.

Anthony Troon, The Scotsman

David Hockney & Stephen Spender in China.

The main news is that both of them caught bronchial ailments and so Hockney was unable to fulfil his vow to find the Chinese equivalent of Bradford. According to Spender, "David sees Bradford in everything. It is the criterion against which all else must be judged." In China he found

*that "some places were more like
Bradford than others."*

Stephen Pile, Sunday Times

To go up so far that there is no down is
still one of my dreams of heaven.

Meanwhile, as always, there is poetry
enough in the here and now. All I do for a
living is put words beside each other but I
have been shown wonders without even
asking. With raw egg dropping from
chopsticks into my lap I have looked
down on the North Pole.

Clive James, Observer

*I travel by public transport because that's where
you hear the authentic voice of the people.*

Sir John Junor, Campaign

**Finding yourself is like finding a lavatory in
a strange town: a great relief.**

Tom Crabtree, Cosmopolitan

VICARS

*In his own view the most interesting press
comment on the personality of the new
Archbishop of Canterbury was the description of
him as "a radical conservative, with self-effacing
charisma".*

Clifford Longley, Guardian

I find God very much now in the songs of Noel Coward – "I'll follow my secret heart", "Some day I'll find you".

Father Harry Williams,
Community of the Resurrection

There is nothing wrong with loving material things for materialist reasons; to want a Rolls-Royce because we admire superb designs and high engineering standards is a profoundly Christian thing to do because such ambitions make possible the God-given creativeness which makes all excellence attainable.

Rev. William Oddie, Daily Telegraph

Gary Davies, C of E vicar of St Mary-le-Boltons, Chelsea. Lives in a fabulous vicarage in the Boltons but surprises more traditional parishioners with his Jungian dream analysis workshops held every week in the vestry. Recently joined

the SDP. A parson with an affable,
distinctly informal manner, he never
wears a dog collar except on trains.

Nicholas Coleridge, Standard

WILDLIFE

Lunch at 1 p.m. is usually bread and
cheese, eaten outside. Afterwards I watch
the bees flying in and out of their hive and
try to guess what is going on in their tiny
minds. I turn away, filled with tenderness.

Jocelyn Wilde, Sunday Times Magazine

First let me tell you about the lobster.
My God! What a lobster! never have I
seen such a lobster. It was a Titan, a
Colossus, a Leviathan, a corker of a
lobster, a veritable Behemoth of
swollen flesh encased in dimpled,
wrinkled, crumpled black armour.
There it squatted on the wooden
planks of Oban pier, massy, meaty,
Goliath turned crustacean, a megalith
of clammy corpulence daring you to
think of mayonnaise and maybe a
small green salad on the side.

Sue Arnold, Observer Colour Magazine

I stood there and I watched the rhino and the
rhino watched me. One had a feeling of some
profound form of communication . . .

Laurens Van Der Post, Radio Four

WINE

Cave de Sologny, Pinot de Bourgogne
'76.
The south of Burgundy rising to the
occasion. Vigorous ripe Pinot Noir is
always attractive young, but this really
wants twelve months in the bottle for the
birdsong of last summer to come through
properly.

Hugh Johnson, Sunday Times

Try the Bandol, Chateau des Vannieres 1972
C-B. This red wine comes from the estate of
Mme Boisseaux right on the edge of the
Mediterranean. "It has" said Peter Reynier "an
elegant warm bouquet and leaves a delicious fresh
tang on the palate. Powerful, dark and quite
heady, this is a real Marlon Brando of a wine."

Katie Bourke, 'Decanter'

Californian wines are ripe and smiling; in
contrast to the often timid taste of cheap
European table wines, they come out to greet
you. You can feel the massive handshake,
and hear them call you by your first name.

Hugh Johnson, Sunday Times

I have another mild pastime and that is a
collection of soil and vine clippings from
the major Grand Cru of Burgundy.
Imagine the pleasure and interest that can
be given to those guests who are genuinely
interested in being able to not only taste a
great wine but to be able to compare the soil
in which the vine was grown with its
neighbours, etc. I wonder if any reader
could coin a name for such pastime. But
perhaps I am an eccentric.

R. Rowan, 'Decanter'

Surrounded by such pefection, in the
rich Edwardian red dining-room with
its Crown Derby and fine glass, I was
introduced to a new and indescribable
experience. With the cheese, at dinner
on my second night, we drank

Chateau Latour 1930. I heard the maitre say, ''It's like old lace'', and Clive Gibson likening it to the music of Clemente, and I understood what they meant. I was not enjoying the taste of an excellent claret, I had discovered a new level of appreciation, a new form of communication for me, the communication which this wine demands is exactly the same as that which you get from great music or great poetry.

Lord Snowdon, Vogue

WOMEN

Lavender Jane Loves Women is a classic of women's liberation music. A lavender-sleeved album of nursery rhymes, yells, reworked Balkan folk tunes – sweet songs about being a woman and a lesbian – it first came to Britain from the USA in 1974 and had a tremendous influence on women's music here.

Angela Phillips/Jill Nicholls, Guardian

A hat is not essential. It is an accessory. But it is also a statement. When a woman wears a hat her body tenses. her femininity is immediately enhanced. She is aware of herself, of her beauty, of how she looks. She immediately feels better about herself.

David Shilling, Woman's Journal

"Making dinner," I said, "may well be the root cause of female paranoia. But you have to remember that dinner can also be an aggression, a penetration, if you like. It doesn't have to be a passive serving-up of the self. Cannibalism is the bottom line of love. Dinner is also a political situation. Historically, it has always been rigidly structured in terms of precedence. It is place, presence, status, not pot roast, that you serve up. When you break bread with someone, it crumbles into possibility."

Anatole Broyard, New York Times

China's Ming tombs were the place where Lynda Birke and Katy Gardner first discussed the possibility of collaborating on a book on pre-menstrual tension.

Katy Gardner, Morning Star

Anita Roddick, *owner of The Body Shops: "Just before setting out for a party, I soak a tiny piece of cotton wool in essential oil and tuck it into the crease in the upper part of my ear. The perfume lingers all night long without fading. If my skin is looking ghastly the next morning, I liquidise an avocado with a whole lettuce and spread some of the mixture on my face, while relaxing in a warm bath. it's fantastic!"*

Cosmopolitan

EPILOGUE

There is not need to differentiate between an apple and a nipple. Despite more than one level of common characteristics, despite their over-lapping connotations, their denotations are worlds apart, and will always remain worlds apart. True, both consist of organic matter. True, both are '-pples' with a vowel preceding. But there's lots of organic matter in this world, and there are lots of '-les', not all of which can etymologically be shown to be diminutives: 'nipple' may, originally, have been one, whereas 'apple' can't. As for the common double 'p', it means as little, i.e. nothing. In short, with all their common traits, the concepts behind the two words can never be mistaken for each other: there'll never be a nipple which anybody will consider an apple, or vice versa.

Hans Keller

Happy Christmas, Happy
Birthday! Judith

TO SHOPS

UP

TRE

DOWN
THEATRE